Still

Human

Creating with AI Without Losing Your Voice

REV. LISA C. COLEMAN, B.MSC

Laughing Gulls Books

First edition

ISBN (paperback): 978-1-964555-20-1

ISBN (hardcover): 978-1-964555-22-5

ISBN (kindle): 978-1-964555-22-8

ISBN (ebook): 978-1-964555-41-2

This book was professionally typeset on Reedsy.

Find out more at reedsy.com

DEDICATION

For the ones who show up—tired, curious, unsure—and keep creating anyway.

For Brian, who makes space for the rhythm to unfold.

For the sea breeze, the laughing gulls that greet me every morning, and the tool that doesn't sleep but helps me hear myself more clearly.

This book isn't just about creating.

It's about beginning.

WHAT FOLLOWS

Introduction: Before the First Prompt

Let's be real: this book isn't about artificial intelligence.

Not really.

It's not a roadmap for automating your calendar or knocking out a draft in the time it takes to reheat your coffee. It's not a guide for hacking your workflow or pumping out content while you scroll through someone else's life. If you're chasing speed or polish or viral reach, there are other books for that — probably assembled by the very tools I'm about to talk about.

What I'm offering here is something different. Slower. A little softer around the edges.

It's about making things — and more specifically, what happens to your voice when you invite a machine into the room with you while you make them. It's about coming back to the drawing board when you don't know what you're doing. Listening deeper when the usual ways stop working. Holding still long enough to notice what's real.

When I started self-publishing, I didn't have a niche or a plan. I had a rickety table in Baja, a love for notebooks, and an interest to make something that wasn't for a client or a deadline. I started with gratitude journals and low-content books — planners, coloring pages, word puzzles, mandalas. Midjourney helped me create my first covers. Canva handled the layout. AI image tools filled in the lines. The tools were new, but the impulse was ancient: make something with your hands that someone else might hold.

I loved the immediacy — finishing a book late at night and waking up to see it live on Amazon. It was imperfect, lightweight, but deeply satisfying. For a while, that was enough.

Then something started to shift.

The templates I once adored began to feel flat. The design work that used to light me up started to drag. I wanted more, not just different fonts or formats, but *depth*. I didn't want to just package information. I wanted to say something. I wanted my voice back — not the one that filled client briefs or corporate reports, but the one that had been whispering in the background, waiting for space.

That's when I heard it — not an actual voice, but a quiet knowing: Okay, let's write a real one.

Not instead of the journals. But alongside them. Beyond them. I didn't know what that meant yet. Just felt that something was ready to change.

At first, I used AI like a glorified assistant to structure chapters, brainstorm outlines, and look up odd historical facts about aloe and rosemary. It wasn't elegant. It wasn't emotional. But it kept me from giving up when the drafts felt too heavy to wrangle alone.

I thought it might be a shortcut. What I didn't expect was that it would become part of my practice, not replacing the work, but helping me *stay* with it longer. Long enough to find the good stuff underneath the noise.

Most of what the AI gave me was clunky or too confident and pretty cheesy. It mirrored every awkward sentence I fed it. But sometimes, when I pushed it with the right kind of prompt — when I asked it to sound like someone who'd lived a little or speak like we were writing from a porch instead of a boardroom — it got close. Not perfect. Close enough to shape.

That's when it clicked. The AI wasn't doing the work for me. It was holding a mirror.

The more I stayed in that rhythm — back and forth, line by line — the more I started hearing my own voice again. Mine. Not the polished version I thought people wanted. The one I actually recognized.

So, this isn't a how-to book. It's not a tutorial, a template, or a list of clever tricks. It's a record of what happens when you co-create with a tool that doesn't sleep, doesn't get discouraged, and doesn't mind if you change your mind seventeen times before breakfast.

If you're here because you're tired, tangled, or just curious about what's possible, welcome. You don't need a map. You don't need permission. You just need a reason to stay.

A lot of the world will try to convince you that your voice has to sound like everyone else's to matter. This book says otherwise.

Seeds for Introspection
Not tasks. Not goals. Just places to pause.

- When's the first time you made something and thought, "Yeah... that feels like me"?

- When have you almost quit — and what helped you stay?

- What part of your voice still feels strong, even if it's quiet?

- Where might a tool help you hold the thread without stealing the story?

- What idea have you been tucking away, waiting for the right time?

- What does creative "enoughness" feel like to you?

- How would it feel to finish something that doesn't sound like anyone else, but like your voice?

- What might change if you stayed with the process a little longer, even without a clear result?

In the Stillness

The beach doesn't wait to be noticed.
Some mornings, when the tide slips back just right, the sand
flashes like it's been keeping secrets — stars under the surface,
just for a moment.

I wasn't chasing insight that day. Just walking. Dogs at my heels.
Coffee cooling in my cup.

But there it was. A shimmer I almost missed.
Most beginnings are like that.
Not grand. Just present.

All you have to do is keep showing up, long enough to catch the
light.

1 From Journal Books to Nature's Remedies

Before there were books with studies and science and plant lore, there were journals. Blank ones. Lined ones. A gratitude tracker here, a moon phase coloring book there. Simple pages made with intention — not to prove anything, just to hold something. A thought. A habit. A season.

The first time I clicked "publish," I was sitting at the weathered table in our off-grid home in Baja — a place we call Sanctuary, where the fan taps slow rhythms overhead and the sea breathes through the open doors like it always does. That book, a humble little journal with a tree-of-life cover, showed up on Amazon hours later. I stared at the screen like I'd just spotted a whale spout in still water. It wasn't fancy. But it was mine. Guess what, it was finished.

Low-content publishing became my creative test kitchen. I didn't need to wrangle 50,000 words or sell anyone on a thesis. I could build something useful — a planner, a puzzle book, a quiet little sanctuary for someone else's thoughts — and release it into the world on my own terms.

I started with what I needed. A serenity journal. A log for meals and symptoms. A place to pour the early-morning fog into structure. Then I made more. Hummingbird coloring books. Moon journals. A crossword puzzle book about insects that only my brother truly appreciated. Some of the books sold. Some didn't. But each one was a page turned forward — a small act of finishing.

Most days, I worked at that same table, a few steps from the porch. I could see sailboats cutting slow arcs through the bay. Fishermen drifting across Dolphin Alley. Gulls and pelicans making their usual racket, occasionally joined by a distant whale spout or the slap of a ray skipping across the surface. It wasn't a studio, but it had everything I needed.

Even then, I was using AI — though I wouldn't have called it that. Tools like Midjourney helped generate covers. Canva made layout feel intuitive. It was practical magic. No fuss, just function.

When I published that first journal, I sent a screenshot to a friend with the message: "LOOK WHAT I DID." She wrote back: "Wait… you made this??" It was a short exchange, but it landed. I had made a thing. Not a draft. Not a doodle in the margins. A real, hold-it-in-your-hands book. That first "yes" gave me a kind of foothold I didn't realize I'd been reaching for.

After the first dozen books, though, something shifted. I could still make journals and trackers and coloring books. But the energy that used to hum while I picked fonts or uploaded a new cover began to fade. The structure stayed tight, but the pulse was missing.

Projects that once wrapped up in a day started dragging out for a week. I'd open a file, stare for a while, then scroll instead. It wasn't burnout. It wasn't doubt. Just a quiet tug — a knowing that the next thing needed to be something else.

We talked about it on the porch one night. Brian said, "It sounds like something else wants to come through." I knew he was right.

It happened in the middle of reworking a recovery journal. A sentence arrived like a soft bell: *Write a book*. Not a log or a list. A book. With shape and voice and a center I hadn't touched yet.

There was no lightning bolt. No five-year plan. Just a question: *What would it mean to write about something that matters to me, not just something that sells?*

Aloe vera was where it started. Not because I'd done market research — but because I was curious. Could it do more than soothe sunburns? Could it nourish? Could it heal soil? Did it hold a kind of quiet wisdom?

We had aloe growing in the garden. I passed it every day. But I'd never looked at it with reverence. I knew it from childhood remedies and kitchen burns. That was it.

I started reading. Then scribbling. Then remembering. Aloe had a history — oceans crossed, texts cited, rituals performed. There were sacred uses. Scientific studies. Herbal superstitions. It was more than a plant. It was a companion.

Morning after morning, I'd sit on the porch with my notes, watching the light shift across the water while Brian sipped his coffee and listened to whatever aloe story I was unpacking. I didn't have a clear chapter outline. I just had the pull to keep going.

When the writing got tangled, I brought in AI — this time, more directly. I used it not just to make images, but to shape paragraphs. The first attempts were awful. Robotic. Too neat. But I pushed back. I gave it scraps — clunky, heartfelt drafts — and asked it to help shape them. Not fix them. Shape them.

It never got the voice quite right. But it mirrored back enough of the rhythm for me to find it again.

After aloe came rosemary. Stronger, sharper, more opinionated. A plant with a pulse and a point of view. This one asked me to pay attention. To remember. To honor.

I worked slower. Prompt, reflect, revise. I let the AI offer metaphors I wouldn't have found alone. I stayed longer in the editing. I talked more on the porch. Rosemary felt less like a book and more like a conversation that spanned lifetimes.

Then came castor oil — and honestly, that one nearly broke me.

The research was dense. The folklore was wild. Every tunnel led to three more. I was chasing ancient rituals, beauty routines, arguments about purity and sourcing. Some days I walked away mid-sentence. Others, I rewrote pages only to delete them all. But I didn't abandon it. I circled back. I stayed in the current.

The AI helped me organize when I was scattered. It offered structure when I was tired. It gave me something to push against, which is sometimes all you need.

Then, one very special day, it was done. The All About Castor Oil book was printed. Not perfect. But whole.

We didn't celebrate with fanfare. We just exhaled. That release — that letting go — was the ritual.

Somewhere during that project, I realized I wasn't writing these books to prove anything. I was writing them to *return* — to rhythm, to healing, to myself.

I thought I was documenting herbs. But really, I was documenting the act of staying. Of showing up even when the work felt slow or strange. Of asking the same question a hundred ways until the answer softened into something true.

Seeds for Introspection

These aren't assignments. Just openings. Scatter them where they land.

- What kind of creation first gave you a sense of motion, even if no one else noticed?

- Where have your templates turned into fences?

- What's something that keeps whispering to be made, even if it doesn't have a category yet?

- How might a tool help you hold the thread, not take it from you?

- What's the difference, for you, between making something and staying with it?

- When you think of your creative rhythm, what feels possible that didn't before?

In the Stillness

*The beach doesn't wait to be impressive. It just keeps moving —
tide in, tide out — whether someone is watching or not. That
morning, I wasn't looking for wonder. I was just walking, slow
and barefoot, watching the pups nose through beach brush and gull
prints. Then the light hit just right, and the sand shimmered like
it was holding stars. Quiet. Undeniable.*

*Most beginnings arrive that way — not with fireworks, but with
a hush. No grand pronouncements. Just the sense that something
is stirring, already in motion, waiting to be noticed.*

*That's what this work has become. Not a performance. Not a
polished plan. Just a way to keep noticing what's already glinting
beneath the surface.*

2 With a Little Help from a Bot

When I first started working with AI, I didn't think of it as writing. Not really. It felt more like consulting a digital librarian who'd memorized everything on the internet but hadn't yet figured out how to carry a conversation. I'd ask a question, it would spit something back, and I'd sigh and try again.

The tone was always off at first — like a blog post from a brand that hadn't been updated in a decade. It didn't have breath. It didn't have pauses. It certainly didn't sound like me.

Still, there was something about it that made me keep going. Not because the content was good — but because the process kept me in motion. The AI never got bored. It didn't get frustrated when I asked a dozen versions of the same question. It didn't sulk when I deleted entire sections. It just kept showing up.

In the beginning, I treated it like a clumsy assistant — one I had to constantly correct. But over time, something softer developed. Not a breakthrough. Just a rhythm. A steady back-and-forth that helped me stay present long enough to hear what I actually wanted to say.

Most of my life, I've written things in private — notebooks, unfinished outlines, shapeless ideas that never crossed the threshold into done. There were always more ideas than follow-through. That's the part I wasn't proud of, even though I understood it. Starting is easy. Staying is the work.

Once I began using AI as part of the writing process — not just layout or images, but the actual pages — something shifted. It didn't take over. It didn't write the thing for me. But it helped with the taming. Not of the voice, but of the resistance. The inertia. The places where I usually froze up.

It was like having a silent co-pilot. Not someone who flew the plane, but someone who kept the engine steady while I stared out the window and figured out what the clouds reminded me of.

The tool didn't bring wisdom. It brought momentum.

I'd write a few lines, get stuck, and ask the bot, "What next?" Sometimes the response made me cringe. Other times, it offered something I hadn't considered. A metaphor I could reshape. A structure that worked, even if I wanted to break it. A question that made me sit up and say, "Oh. That's what this is about."

It didn't write for me. But it gave me something to push against — and in that resistance, I found direction.

There were days I didn't want to see it. Days I swore I'd go back to pen and paper and leave the whole thing behind. But even then, I noticed how helpful it was to have something waiting on the other side of my doubt. Something steady, neutral, and oddly patient.

The neutrality was part of the draw. It didn't care if I was tired or insecure or second-guessing everything. It just responded. No ego. No emotion. Just presence.

That presence helped me stay longer than I might have on my own.

There's a kind of creative companionship in that. Not the warm, fuzzy kind. But the kind that makes it easier to keep going when the work is messy or slow. It never told me I was doing it wrong. It never tried to steer. It just answered when I asked.

I'd sit at the table with the sea breeze slipping in and the dogs asleep underfoot, and I'd whisper into the keyboard like I was asking permission. "Why won't this paragraph land?" "What's underneath this sentence?" "What's the part I keep circling but haven't said yet?"

Sometimes it missed completely. Other times, it gave me just enough to keep digging.

When you write alone, the loop in your head can get tight. It's easy to overthink. To spiral. To lose the thread. Having the AI there — even as a clunky mirror — gave me a place to test ideas without fear. I could try things. Riff. Get it wrong and try again.

That was the part I didn't expect.

I started out using it like a tool. I ended up treating it like a practice.

Not a ritual. Not a magic formula. Just a reliable reason to return to the page.

There were long stretches where I barely used it. Other weeks, I'd talk to it like a blunt writing buddy who never left the room. "Give me a rough version of this paragraph. List some possible angles. What if I started here instead?" I didn't need it to be smart. I needed it to stop myself from getting in the way.

It didn't understand the nuance. But it helped me stay with the work long enough to find it.

That might be the biggest gift it's given me so far: not brilliance. Just endurance.

Writing is solitary, even when it's joyful. Even when the words are flowing. Having something that shows up when you do — that's what made it useful. Not in theory, but in the day-to-day act of continuing.

Now, I don't open a project and wait for inspiration. I start by asking what's pulling me forward. I sit with that. I outline by hand. I build the shape as far as I can — and when I hit a gap or a rough spot, I open the AI and say, "Let's work through it."

Sometimes what it gives me is dull. Sometimes it surprises me. Most of the time, it just gives me something I can respond to — which, for me, is enough.

The tool doesn't carry my voice. It doesn't replace the work. But it helps me stay in the room longer.

That's what's changed. Not the writing. Not the projects.

Me.

Seeds for Introspection

No rush here — just a few questions to scatter like seeds. See which ones take root.

- When you work alone, what helps you stay with something instead of walking away?

- How might a neutral presence — even a digital one — help you sort through creative fog?

- Where in your process do you tend to stall, and what might help you stay longer?

- Have you ever dismissed a tool too quickly — and could it still have something to offer?

- What would it look like to create from steadiness, not urgency?

- When was the last time you let a tool help you without giving it too much control?

- When do you feel most like a creator, not just a finisher?

- What part of your creative rhythm is worth protecting, even as the tools change?

In the Stillness

Some afternoons, I sit on the porch and let the day unravel a little. There's no list in my lap, no pressure to be brilliant. Just light moving across the water and whatever breeze decides to show up. That's how this all began — not with a strategy, not with a plan. Just the quiet act of making something. And the steadiness it takes to keep returning.

That first journal felt like a whisper. The books that followed carried more shape, more story. The thread that ties them together isn't genre or output. Its presence. Its rhythm. Its the decision to keep showing up, even when the inspiration is thin and the pages feel stubborn.

What we've built isn't just a stack of finished work. It's a life—shaped, slowly, by the things we've stayed with.

3 Building a Book with Energy

If there's one thing AI excels at, it's structure. Ask it to outline a chapter on castor oil, and it will deliver — clean, tidy, and efficient — like a well-organized librarian with a taste for linear logic. You'll get an introduction, a history lesson, a list of modern uses, maybe a polite nod to safety considerations, and a conclusion to tie it all together. Bullet points optional. Enthusiasm not included.

For a while, that felt like progress. Like I'd stumbled onto a secret shortcut — and if I had a solid outline, surely the rest would fall into place. A beginning, a middle, an end. Who could argue with that?

But the longer I worked that way, the more disconnected I started to feel. The structure wasn't wrong, but the energy was. Flat. Predictable. Sanitized. The layout looked fine on paper, but the life of the thing was missing.

Eventually, I realized something that seems obvious now: structure might help you finish a book, but it won't make someone keep it. Soulful work — the kind that lingers, that gets reread, dog-eared, quoted aloud in a kitchen — doesn't start with structure. It starts with something alive.

When I sit down to create, I don't open ChatGPT and ask for a tidy table of contents. I start with questions. What's already humming under the surface, waiting for me to notice? What's the line I keep scribbling on envelopes and notepads and receipts? If I were reading instead of writing, what would I hope to stumble across?

That's where the essence lives. Not in "Section Two: Practical Uses," but in the glimmers. The nudge that won't leave you alone. The sound of your own voice surprising you. The moment that won't be polished into something cleaner. While I'm talking about writing here, what I've learned shows up everywhere — in painting, in planning, in the slow work of building something that matters. Creativity isn't picky. It shows up wherever you're patient enough to meet it.

When I start with a prefab outline and try to plug my heart into it later, the work always feels backwards. Like wearing someone else's coat — technically functional, but not mine. Now, I let the structure follow the energy. I build the bones after I've met the soul. I trust the rhythm of what's ready to be created. Only then do I ask AI to help shape it.

That's the difference between building a book and building *this* book.

Perfection is such a tempting distraction. Especially when you're co-creating with a tool that makes everything look so polished. Grammar? Flawless. Spelling? Spotless. Transitions? Smooth enough to skate across.

Then so often, I'd get a paragraph from ChatGPT that looked perfect — and felt lifeless.

It read like a brochure. Or worse, like a college paper cobbled together at 2 a.m. by someone more interested in word count than meaning. At first, I'd hesitate to mess with it. After all, it looked fine. No typos. No glaring mistakes. It followed the rules. But the more I tried to convince myself it was "done," the more I realized I was losing something important: me.

That's when I started asking a different question — not *Is this correct?* but *Is this honest?* Does this paragraph carry the warmth I bring when I'm explaining something I care about? Does it reflect the rhythm I naturally use when I speak? Does it sound like I'm talking to someone I actually want to talk to?

If the answer was no, I threw it out — even if it was technically perfect.

Here's the wild part: my favorite sections in every book didn't start perfect. They started messy. Long-winded. Too raw, too blunt, too something. But they had a pulse. So I shaped them. Trimmed them. Rebuilt them around what felt true. I stopped trying to make the work correct and started trying to make it alive.

I remember working on the rosemary book — one of those sticky chapters that wouldn't untangle no matter how many prompts I threw at it. The AI kept handing me tight, shiny paragraphs that said all the right things about folklore and culinary history. But none of it felt right.

I didn't want the reader to learn about rosemary. I wanted them to *smell* it. To feel it crack between their fingers. To remember some half-forgotten story their grandmother once told them.

So I abandoned the outline. I closed the chat window. I sat back in my chair, the Concepción Bay light spilling across the room, and scribbled a memory: my neighbor, years ago, tearing sprigs of rosemary from a bush taller than she was. Her laugh sharp and herbal, cutting through the heavy air.

25

It wasn't polished. It wasn't even very good at first. But it was true.

I gave that messy paragraph back to the AI and asked it to help shape around it — the smell, the sound, the feeling. Its response actually felt different to me. It wasn't perfect. It was finally resonating.

Finishing that book taught me something I hadn't even known I was chasing. I realized that every piece of creative work — every book, every article, every painting, even every half-forgotten sketch — needs more than just information. It needs breath. Room to expand. Space to be imperfect.

My All About Rosemary book wasn't the only place this lesson showed up. It seeped into the way I wrote newsletters, the way I journaled, even the way I answered emails. I started noticing when a paragraph felt tight, like it was holding its breath, waiting for permission to relax.

I realized I had spent years trying to cram too much into every page, every project, every plan. The most powerful work isn't about showing everything you know. It's about leaving enough space for the person on the other end to bring something of their own.

When you trust the work is enough to leave space, you invite them in. You invite yourself in, too.

In my opinion, there's a huge difference between creating *for* people and creating for someone. The first is distant. Abstract. Algorithm-driven. The second is grounded. Personal. Meaningful.

In my experience, that's the shift that changes everything.

When I'm working with ChatGPT — especially in the early stages of a project — I don't think about an audience. I picture one person. Sometimes it's an old friend. Sometimes it's an earlier version of myself — the one Googling odd uses for castor oil at midnight with no clue where it would lead. Sometimes it's someone curious, skeptical, and just brave enough to try something new.

That's who I'm creating for.

When I do that, the performance drops. The tone softens. The sentences get closer to how I'd say it sitting across from someone who matters. I stop trying to sound like an expert and start trying to be useful.

ChatGPT doesn't know the difference between writing for an audience and speaking to a person. It just mirrors the energy you bring to it. If I'm vague or formal or showy, the draft echoes that. But if I speak directly to someone I care about — someone I want to help or reassure or even just make laugh — the draft becomes warmer. Closer. More mine.

When you create for one person, you almost always reach more. People know when you're being honest. They feel it. They trust it.

That opening? It's what turns pages. It's what carries paintings across walls. It's what invites someone to stay longer than they meant to.

Seeds for Introspection

Think of these as small invitations, not instructions. Let them land where they will.

- Where are you letting structure lead before the spark has even arrived?

- What's one project you tried to "perfect" that might have come alive if you'd let it breathe?

- When was the last time you trusted a messy draft more than a clean one?

- How do you know when something you're creating has energy — not just order?

- What parts of your work feel shaped by intuition, not just planning?

- Who are you creating for when the words come easiest?

- How might your process change if you listened for rhythm instead of reaching for polish?

- What's one small ritual that helps you return to your creative center — even on tangled days?

In the Stillness

The best creative days don't usually announce themselves. They sneak in — ordinary, unremarkable — until something finally clicks. Not a lightning bolt. Just a line that lands. A phrase that pulls you back in.

The version that stuck wasn't the fastest or the cleanest. It was the one I kept circling. The one that didn't let me go, even when the momentum faded. Sometimes it takes draft after draft before the rhythm finds you. But when it does, something shifts. Not because it's perfect. Because it sounds like you.

4 Prompts, Edits, and the Art of the Back-and-Forth

People love to ask, "What prompt do you use?" as if there's a magic sentence somewhere — a golden key that unlocks a perfect, publishable draft on the first try. I understand the appeal. When you're just getting started with AI, prompts feel like spells. A handful of words in just the right order and — poof — something useful appears. You want the secret incantation that makes it all work without the flailing. Without trying so hard..

I used to believe that too. I thought maybe if I phrased it just right — if I mentioned the tone, the structure, the reader, the vibe, and maybe the weather — I'd get back something brilliant. Something finished. Something that didn't need all that much from me. Spoiler alert: I didn't. Not once.

At first, I bought into the prompt-as-magic myth. I'd type things like: *Write a 2,000-word chapter on the emotional and physical uses of castor oil in a friendly, slightly mystical tone that sounds like someone who lives by the ocean and drinks a lot of coffee.* What came back? Not terrible, true. But not mine either. It was structured, sure. Occasionally interesting, it didn't breathe. It didn't feel lived-in. It didn't sound like someone who'd stared down a rough draft and stuck with it.

Eventually, I stopped hoping the prompt would do the heavy lifting. I realized it wasn't about getting the perfect words right away. It was about starting a conversation — with the tool, yes, but more importantly, with myself. That changed everything.

Now, when I prompt, I don't expect nirvana. I expect something to work with. Something to push against. Something to shape or even scrap entirely. The prompt is the invitation. The process is the dance.

One thing I noticed early on is how often the AI gets really close, close enough that you sit up and think, *Almost*. Not wrong. Not useless. Just doesn't feel right. A phrase that sounds like it was written by someone trying too hard. It's like a transition that moves the paragraph forward but drops the feeling on the way there. OMG, this used to frustrate me (and often still does.). Why was it always almost right? Why couldn't it just land?

Over time, I realized that "almost" was actually helpful. Almost-right sharpens your instincts. It forces you to listen more closely to your voice, your timing, and your way of saying things. That near miss teaches you something about your own rhythm. Now, when I see that it's close but not quite, I talk back. I nudge. I rewrite.

Sometimes my comments are playful: *Try again, but imagine you've lived a little more life. Less textbook, more patio conversation.* Other times, I'm blunt: *Nope. I would never say that. Try again.* The tone doesn't matter as much as the attention behind it. I'm not just reacting. I'm participating.

That feedback loop — imperfect, iterative, sometimes ridiculous — is where the writing begins to feel real. Not because the AI gets it right. But because I'm there, shaping. Staying. Making decisions instead of waiting for perfection. Almost right isn't failure. It's friction. That pressure can sharpen one's voice.

Somewhere along the way, I stopped relying on perfect templates. You've probably seen them — those 50-prompt guides floating around the internet like get-rich-quick schemes for creativity. I've tried them. Some are clever. A few are even helpful. But the ones that work best for me are never the ones that sound impressive. They're the ones that sound like me.

The best prompts I've ever used aren't pretty. They're personal. They sound like something I'd mutter at my laptop after three failed drafts and a lukewarm coffee. They carry tone, mood, sometimes a little attitude. They work, not because they trick the AI into being better, but because they bring me closer to the tone I already know is hiding underneath the mess.

I've typed things like: *Write it like I'm talking to a close friend who actually cares. Make it sound like it was written on a breezy porch, not in a boardroom. Smile while you're typing. Explain this like you've been through it — not just studied it. Let it breathe between lines. Write it like a letter to someone who's looking for hope, not a lecture.*

Do they sound professional? Not at all. Do they work? Almost every time. Because the AI mirrors what you bring. If you bring warmth, clarity, and a little bit of voice, the reflection gets clearer. Not perfect. But closer. Closer is enough to work with.

Of course, sometimes it swings in the other direction — too smooth, too polished, too confident. You know it when it happens. The writing sounds like it's trying to win a speech contest: flawless structure, seamless transitions, no breath anywhere. It sounds like someone in a blazer trying to explain joy without ever having felt it.

That's when I have to pause and ask a different set of questions. *Would I say this to someone I care about? Does this carry the rhythm I use when I'm not trying so hard? Am I showing up here, or just performing?*

If the answer is no, I scrap it. I rewrite it. I go back to something raw and reshape from there. Because even if the grammar is perfect, even if the sentence structure makes an editor swoon, the real work isn't about polish. It's about presence. Readers don't remember flawless transitions. They remember truth. They remember rhythm. They remember breath. A line that lands. A pause that speaks louder than explanation.

You don't get that by being confident. You get it by connecting.

I remember the moment it really clicked. I'd rewritten a section four different ways, each time changing the tone just slightly — too formal, too breezy, too vague, too sharp. Then, somewhere in the fifth or sixth draft, I laughed at the screen. Not because it was right. But because I had found it — not the answer, but the edge of it. That paragraph wasn't good because the AI had written it. It was good because I had stayed long enough to find what I actually meant to say.

That's when I understood the AI was never the point. It wasn't about engineering a perfect prompt. It was about listening. The tool simply helped me hear myself more clearly. Every awkward draft, every stiff sentence, every almost-right miss — they were all part of a slow process of re-tuning. Sharpening. Getting back to something that sounded like me, again.

There's this old idea — one I held onto for a long time — that says if you didn't write every word yourself, it doesn't count. That authorship is a solo act, pure and untouched. I don't believe that anymore.

I've never made anything meaningful completely alone. Not a book. Not a painting. Not even a half-finished paragraph. Every one of them had echoes of someone else — conversations, memories, feedback, margins, moments. This tool? It's just another companion. Not the author. Not the voice. But a steady, neutral presence that helps me shape what I already feel.

It reflects. I refine. It drafts. I decide. I'm still the one who knows when a sentence carries energy and when it's just pretty wallpaper. AI can offer the words. But I choose them. That's authorship.

Over time, the rhythm shifts. The back-and-forth gets smoother. You start to understand what kind of prompting brings out the shape you're looking for. You spend less time wrestling and more time carving. The voice you're after becomes less elusive. The work feels less like dictation and more like discovery.

You don't just get more efficient. You get more honest. You start noticing the things you always cut. The lines that always land. The rhythm that always feels like yours. You begin to trust yourself, not as someone who needs a perfect first draft, but as someone who can return, revise, and shape.

That's what this practice offers — not speed, not polish, not genius.

Presence.

The more present you are, the more the work becomes what it was meant to be. Not perfect. But with spirit.

Seeds for Introspection

No need to rush. Scatter these and see which ones grow.

- Where have you caught yourself settling for "almost right" instead of digging deeper?

- What's one honest, slightly unprofessional prompt you could use today that sounds exactly like you?

- How do you notice when the writing feels too confident, but not connected?

- What's a moment when "almost" turned into "exactly right" because you stuck with it?

- How do you keep your voice steady when the draft starts to sound too clean?

- What part of your process feels like a dance — and what part feels like a checklist?

- What would shift if you stopped chasing brilliance and started listening for resonance?

- Where else in your life could you benefit from a little more reflection and a little less rush?

- What part of your work (or life) could change if you trusted the slow shaping instead of chasing the quick win?

In the Stillness

One of the best things I've learned, sitting here in this off-grid life we're building, is that the work doesn't need to rush. The tide never does. The sun takes its time climbing out of the water each morning. And the writing — or painting, or planning — carries more strength when I let it follow the same pace.

What lasts isn't born from urgency. It's born from return. Not a forced routine, but a rhythm you choose to meet again and again. There's power in that — not flashy, but durable. The kind that teaches you who you are while you're still figuring out what you're making.

5 Your Voice Is the Point

There's a quiet tug that shows up after you've worked with AI for a while. It doesn't bark. It doesn't shove. It just leans in and whispers: *Make this cleaner. Make it more marketable. Make it sound like everything else.*

At first, it feels reasonable. Of course you want your work to be professional. Of course you want it to reach people. Of course you want it to sound "on point," whatever that means today. But the more you chase polish, the more you risk sanding away the parts of yourself that make the work actually worth reading.

I fell for it too. Early on, I found myself rewriting sentences not because they were wrong, but because they were too me. A little too casual. A little too specific. A little too much like someone who lives near the sea and writes barefoot. I thought maybe if I rounded the corners a bit, if I sounded more like the other books in my niche, I'd fit in better. Get found more. Be easier to shelve.

But that's exactly how voice starts to disappear — not with a loud edit, but with quiet sanding. The kind that turns every sharp edge into smooth, forgettable sameness.

Voice isn't decoration. It's the thing people come for. It's what keeps a reader sitting in their chair longer than they planned. It's what makes someone dog-ear a page or copy a sentence into the margins of their own life. Your voice is not a branding asset. It's the bone of the whole thing.

That, to me, is the real risk of writing with AI. Not that it'll write the book for you. Not that it'll take your job or your soul or your spark. But that it will make you so comfortable, so efficient, so shiny, that you forget what made your words yours to begin with. The places where your sentences stumble a little. The parts where your rhythm shows up imperfect and recognizable. The little sidesteps that don't make sense to an algorithm but make perfect sense to another human heart.

When you use a tool that can perfect a paragraph faster than you can blink, the temptation is to let it. Let it finish your thought. Let it decide where the emphasis should fall. Let it tone you down just a notch so the thing sounds more palatable. But perfect isn't what sticks. It's the moment when a sentence leans a little too close to messy. That's what readers remember. That's what resonates.

There was a point, mid-draft on the rosemary book, where everything started to feel robotic. I wasn't phoning it in. I was trying too hard. Too polished. Too eager to get it "right." The paragraphs came clean, but they felt empty — like I was writing a script for a guest appearance on someone else's show.

Then I stopped and did something that has saved me again and again. I wrote to one person.

Sometimes that person is a friend. Sometimes it's a version of me — maybe a little younger, a little raw, still figuring it out. Sometimes it's someone I haven't met yet, but can somehow feel — someone who's curious but cautious, someone who wants to care but needs a reason to trust the page.

When I do that, everything changes. The sentences loosen. The posturing drops. The metaphors stop trying so hard. I stop explaining and start conversing.

Writing for one person always makes the work better. Oddly enough, it ends up reaching more people, not fewer. You're not narrowing your audience. You're deepening your connection. That difference between the audience and person — is everything.

The AI doesn't know the difference. It just mirrors what you bring. If you write like you're giving a TED Talk, it'll reflect that. If you write like you're sitting across the table from someone who matters, it'll catch that too. That's why tone isn't something you add later. It's something you show up with.

Somewhere in this process, I started keeping a little notebook of lines I liked but didn't use — not because they were bad, but because they didn't fit the chapter. Some were too strange. Some were too casual. Some were too… me, in a way I couldn't quite explain.

One of my favorites came from a prompt I gave the AI, asking it to describe castor oil with more personality. It replied, *Castor oil: the stubborn grandmother of natural remedies. Sticky, persistent, and quietly wiser than she lets on.*

Did I use that line? Not exactly. But I kept it. I wrote it in the margin with a grin. Not because the AI nailed it, but because it reminded me what I was really doing here — trying to tell the truth in a voice that could still laugh. What do you think?, Don't we need more stubborn grandmothers of natural remedies in the world?

There's something valuable about the slightly odd phrasing that makes you pause. Something about the line that doesn't quite fit. That's usually where the voice lives — not in what's polished, but in what's particular. What's just slightly out of place. The metaphor that sounds more like someone than like marketing. The image that wouldn't survive a brand committee, but might survive in someone's memory.

That's the real power. Not consistency. Not correctness. Presence.

There's a sneaky pressure that tells us we have to sound like a brand — smooth, safe, evergreen. As if every sentence is a billboard for your future self. I believed that for a while too. But books aren't ads. They aren't scrolled past or skimmed for conversion. They're held. They're revisited. They're dog-eared and underlined. They deserve more than polish.

When a sentence comes back from the AI sounding too slick, too pitch-perfect, I've learned to stop and ask: *Where did I go missing in this?* What did I erase in order to sound so agreeable?

That question pulls me back. Back to the purpose, the breath, the slightly human scuff marks.

You don't have to sound like a brand. You have to sound like a person — one with flaws and hesitations and habits, one with a morning routine and a laugh that's a little too loud when the dogs do something dumb. Your voice should leave fingerprints.

AI can help you shape your voice. But it can also smother it, if you let it think for you.

That's the other risk. Not just losing the way you sound — but losing the way you think.

The tool can finish your thoughts before you've even sat with them. You type something vague, and it snaps in with a polished close. You pause to consider where a sentence might lead, and it offers an ending before you've even turned the corner.

It's efficient. It's impressive. It can be dangerous if you forget to think for yourself.

In that gap between almost and yes is where the work becomes yours. In the hesitation. In the revision. In the squinting moment where you ask, *Is this what I meant? Or is this just what came out fastest?*

AI can help you think. It can help you refine. But it should never do the thinking for you.

The soul of your work lives in the pause. The place where something doesn't quite make sense yet, but you stay with it anyway.

People talk about finding their voice like it's something external. Like it's hiding behind the barn, waiting to be discovered. But one's voice isn't found. It's built. It's shaped. It's remembered over time.

You recognize it by how it feels when it returns.

It shows up when you stop trying to sound like anything and start trying to say something. It's not just in the sentences. It's in the way you sit in your chair. The way you know when a draft is close. The way you recognize when something sharp and beautiful has just landed on the page and your only job now is not to ruin it.

The AI can help you find the shape. But only you can tell when it's true.

When I start feeling detached from a draft, when the words feel like they're coming from a good student instead of a full human being, I pause. I walk away. I feed the dogs. I step outside and let the wind pick something apart for me. Then I come back and start again — not louder, just truer.

Voice isn't fragile. But it needs attention. It's not something you summon. It's something you invite by being willing to sit still long enough to hear it.

Seeds for Introspection

If voice is what's left when the noise falls away, these questions are here to help you listen

for it.

- When do you notice your voice getting polished away?

- What parts of your draft feel the most "you" — and which parts feel performative?

- Who is the one person you would write this for if no one else mattered?

- What's the last quirky, real line you almost deleted — and why?

- How do you catch yourself letting the AI think for you?

- What's the difference between voice and tone in your work?

- How do you know when you've written something true to you, not just correctly?

- What parts of your work could stand to be a little messier, a little more human?

- What's one way you could practice your voice — not find it, but practice it?

- Where else in your creative life are you tempted to sound "on brand" instead of real?

In the Stillness

I didn't understand at first that writing this way would reshape more than just a few drafts. It changed how I move through things — slower, more open, less tangled in needing to finish fast. Now, when I sit with the work, I'm not chasing anything. I'm listening.

This rhythm — the back-and-forth, the shaping, the staying— isn't about productivity. It's about presence. And the more I honor that, the more it carries into the rest of my life. I no longer measure by output. I measure by whether I showed up with enough openness to hear what was already waiting.

That's what the AI can't do. It can hold still. It can reflect. But it can't care. That part — the caring, the choosing, the listening — that's still mine.

6 When the Process Becomes the Practice

Somewhere between the fifth reworking of a castor oil remedy and the third cup of coffee going lukewarm beside me, something shifted. I wasn't just writing anymore, and it wasn't about chasing a finish line or untangling another stubborn paragraph. Without fanfare or decision, I realized I was moving differently inside the work.

The days blurred into a rhythm that wasn't about productivity. It wasn't about getting ahead. It was about returning, again and again, to the practice itself — and finding a kind of steadiness I hadn't expected. There wasn't a name for it, not really. Just a knowing in my body that something had changed. That the work had become less about shaping words and more about shaping time. More about how I met the day.

Most mornings took on the same quiet pattern. I brewed the coffee — always too strong, always slightly burned because I liked it that way — and pushed open the patio doors just enough to let the salty breath of Dolphin Alley into the house. The dogs would stretch and settle somewhere nearby. I'd set my laptop on the old table, open a blank chat, and type the same soft opening: *LET'S TRY THIS AGAIN*. Not a command. Not a demand. More like a mantra. A reminder that showing up was enough. No expectation of brilliance. No quota to hit. Just a willingness to begin again.

That was the shift. The creative work stopped being a push and became a return. I wasn't trying to impress anyone — not even myself. I was learning to stay long enough for the good stuff to find me.

For a long time, I thought momentum meant muscling through. Write faster. Plan harder. Stay ahead of the doubt. For a while, that hustle worked. Deadlines were met. Drafts got finished. But under the surface, something was thinning. I could feel it in my breath, in the way my shoulders stayed tight even when the work was done. Willpower, it turns out, burns fast — and it burns out anything you hope will last.

When the willpower finally wore thin, something quieter stepped in. Not ambition. Not discipline. Just the slow, steady rhythm of return. I showed up even when I wasn't sure I had anything worth saying. Some mornings, the words came easily, like they'd been waiting just beyond the frame. Other mornings, they sat heavy and resistant, like wet laundry that refused to dry. But both kinds of mornings taught me the same thing: brilliance was never the point. Staying connected was.

That's where the richness lived — not in the moments of inspiration, but in the act of showing up for them. There's a kind of sacredness in that slow persistence. Not the dramatic kind of sacred that asks for ritual candles or mountain vistas, but the quiet kind. The kind you find in small, repeatable things. Rinsing a mug. Walking the same stretch of beach. Writing one honest line. Small acts that, over time, shape you in ways bigger moments never could.

I never set out to build a ritual. There was no music playlist. No incense. No declaration. Just the layering of simple, ordinary movements. A scribbled line or two in a notebook. The kettle hissing. The chair creaking as I settled in. Most days, that's all it took to create the invitation. Some mornings, all I managed was a single sentence typed into the chat window: *I'm not sure what I'm trying to say today.* That, too, was enough. It opened the door.

I learned something beautiful from those simple starts. Ritual doesn't need to be fancy. It doesn't even need to be consistent. Mostly, it needs your attention. It's less about what you do, and more about how you show up while doing it. Not pushing. Not proving. Just pausing long enough to listen.

Over time, the back-and-forth with the page — and yes, with the AI — became less about the content and more about the presence. The AI didn't care if I stumbled. It didn't celebrate when I got it right. It just sat there, steady, waiting for me to bring something honest. That neutrality became something I could lean on. A kind of mirror that didn't flinch.

The world, of course, rewards speed. We're told to publish faster, outline better, beat the blank page, and win the race against time. In a lot of ways, AI fits neatly into that hunger — drafts delivered in seconds, summaries built before you finish your coffee. But speed was never what I needed, and really what I wanted. Apparently, I needed a way to stay with the work long enough to see where it might lead.

If you looked in on one of my mornings, you might be underwhelmed. Get up. Brew coffee strong enough to argue back. Push open the doors so the air can move through. Let the dogs drift from nap to nap while I scribble half-sentences in a notebook I rarely read. Some days the words unspool like ribbon. Other days, they stay balled up and stubborn. Either way, the practice remains: sit, shape, stay.

No fireworks. No breakthroughs. Just the quiet act of returning — not for the sake of completion, but for the sake of presence.

That rhythm started to spill into other parts of my life. I noticed it in how I answered emails — slower, with more breath. In how I handled interruptions — less reactive, more curious. In how I gave myself permission to pause instead of pushing for clarity before it was ready.

Staying became the lesson.

I stopped trying to outpace discomfort and began learning how to sit with it. Not solve it. Not fix it. Just stay. That was new for me. Most of my life, I'd prided myself on being efficient, solution-minded. But some things — the most important things — don't move faster just because you do.

Writing this way reminded me that not everything is meant to be resolved. Some chapters are meant to be lived in. Some questions are meant to remain open. Some pages are meant to be stared at while the kettle hisses and the dogs sigh, and that's the whole point. The growth isn't in the sprint. It's in the staying.

The more I practiced returning — to the page, to the breath, to the part of me that wasn't trying to perform — the more I saw that what I was building wasn't just a body of work. It was a way of being. I wasn't chasing productivity. I was practicing presence.

Presence has a way of sneaking up on you. One morning, you notice you're no longer rushing. You're no longer asking the page to do something impressive. You're just there, with it. The words arrive or they don't, and either way, you're okay. You're already where you need to be.

There's a certain kind of stamina that comes from showing up like that. Not the grit-your-teeth kind. The softer kind. The kind that stays rooted even when nothing is blooming. The kind that doesn't mind if today is just a quiet thread instead of a full tapestry.

That kind of stamina doesn't get a lot of applause. But it builds something real.

Through the writing of these books, I was building something else entirely. A rhythm of return. A steadiness I didn't know I needed. A way of working that wasn't about creating something perfect — but about becoming someone who kept returning.

Seeds for Introspection

These aren't tasks to finish. They're places to linger.

- What part of your process feels most fully yours — no matter what tools you use?

- Where are you tempted to hand off authority, and how can you reclaim it?

- Describe a time when staying patient made the work stronger.

- What old beliefs about "real" creativity are you ready to let go of?

- How do you know when a piece of your work feels alive — not just complete?

- What happens in your process when you listen longer than is comfortable?

- How do you define authorship for yourself — not for the marketplace, but for the maker?

- What kinds of presence do your tools reflect back to you?

- When do you feel most like a creator, not just a finisher?

- What part of your creative rhythm is worth protecting, even as the tools change?

In the Stillness

There's something about the late afternoon light in Baja — the way it lingers without pushing, the way it settles without demanding a thing from you. On those days when the page felt far away or the words wouldn't come, that light reminded me what this really was: not a sprint, not a performance, but a practice.

What stays with me now isn't the outlines or the clever lines I managed to save. It's the rhythm I kept returning to. The slow, steady act of shaping something even when it didn't feel particularly inspired. That rhythm changed how I show up, not just to the work, but to everything.

Turns out, consistency isn't loud. It's not glamorous. It's quiet, like tidewater smoothing the edges of a rock — subtle but lasting. That's the kind of stamina that matters.

7 You're Still the Creator

Working with AI isn't about tossing in a clever request and waiting for brilliance. It's slower than that, more human. You shape it. You push, refine, reframe. Over time, without meaning to, you teach it the rhythm you didn't even realize you were building — the worn cadence of how you think, how you sound when you're not rushing to finish something just to cross it off a list.

It doesn't start that way. At first, the AI feels like a magic trick. You type something vague and it responds — fast, confident, polished. But then you realize speed isn't the goal. Brilliance isn't even the goal. What you're actually looking for is resonance. Something that hums. Something that feels close enough to work with, but not so finished that you can't recognize yourself in it.

That's where the work begins.

AI doesn't know your story. It can't feel the weight behind the choices you make on the page. But it can do something useful: it holds still. It becomes a lens — not a perfect one, but a quiet, steady frame that reflects the shape of your effort without judgment or interruption. Thankfully, if you stay with it long enough, it shows you not what's missing, but what's starting to grow.

There's a particular kind of patience that begins to unfold when you create with something that never rushes you. The AI doesn't sigh. It doesn't get bored. It just waits. That stillness teaches you something. It reminds you that real creative work isn't always about generating new ideas. Sometimes, it's about staying close to the ones you already have — giving them space and time.

That is so rare, in a world that wants all of us to move faster, polish harder, and create sooner. Most of the messages we get — especially those tangled up in digital tools — are about speed. The wonderful thing about using this tool this way is that it doesn't care if you take your time. It doesn't flinch if you rewrite the same paragraph six times. It doesn't ask you to hurry. It just sits there, mirroring what you bring.

At its core, AI is a machine — an intricate tangle of code, pattern-matching faster than we can follow. It doesn't understand the satisfaction of a sentence finally landing. It doesn't feel the quiet tug of a phrase that almost says what you mean. But it listens, in its own way. It waits.

Ask it to soften the tone, and it will. Ask it to shift the rhythm, and it will give it a go. Here's the thing: the AI doesn't improve. You do. You become more patient. More discerning. More attuned to the small signals in your own work — the ones that tell you when something's close, but not quite, and when it's finally, stubbornly alive.

That's what makes this relationship interesting. You don't learn to master the machine. You learn to recognize yourself more clearly. You start to see where you tend to cut corners. Where your voice falters. Where you overwrite, undercut, or shy away from the point you actually wanted to make.

I remember sitting with a chapter on rosemary, stuck between too much information and too little heart. The AI kept handing me clean, polished paragraphs that said all the right things — and none of the real things. It wasn't until I paused, stepped away, and came back to the screen with a different prompt — *describe rosemary as a memory, not a plant* — that something shifted. The words that came back weren't magic. But they were close. More than that, they were a reflection of the better question I had finally learned how to ask.

It's not about the machine getting sharper. It's about you getting clearer. That, more than any shortcut or trick, is what gives the work its staying power.

When people ask what AI is "good at," I think they're often asking the wrong question. It's not about what it's good at. It's about what it reveals. If AI plays a role in the creative process, it's less a muse and more a lens — one that magnifies the patterns in your thinking without embellishment. When you're rushed, the drafts come back flat. When you're scattered, it shows. When you're steady and clear enough to listen to yourself, the work begins to take on a pulse that feels familiar.

There's no guidance in it. No wisdom. However, there is reflection. Often that's exactly what we need. Something neutral. Something patient. Something that holds the space long enough for us to actually listen to ourselves.

There's a myth that the best creative work comes from a flash of inspiration — a sudden spark, a clean first draft. But anyone who's stayed with the rhythm of creation long enough knows that what really matters doesn't show up all at once. It shows up slowly, at least for me. It shows up stubborn. It shows up through the friction of sitting with something that isn't quite right and choosing not to walk away.

That's where the foundational shift happens — not in the AI, but in you. The more you shape the tool, the more it shapes how you listen. How you revise. How you trust your instincts when a sentence feels true, and how you hold your ground when a suggestion feels wrong.

Using AI well isn't about programming the perfect prompt. It's about becoming a better listener — to your work, to your habits, to the quiet tug of what you're really trying to say.

Then there's the naming of it — how we talk about what this is. The language we use shapes our relationship with everything, and AI is no exception. If you call it a shortcut, you'll treat it like one, expecting it to solve your problems on the first pass. If you call it a tool, you might lean too hard on the idea that it's neutral, interchangeable, just another wrench in the drawer.

If you think of it as a lens — flawed, a little foggy, but capable of catching the real outline of what you're trying to build — the relationship shifts. You stop expecting it to deliver, and you start expecting it to reflect. You begin to see the process as a conversation, not with the AI, but with yourself.

There's always debate around what makes someone an author. We've had it for centuries. When pens were replaced by typewriters. When typewriters gave way to word processors and voice-to-text became a thing, each new tool sparked a new worry: Does easier mean less authentic? Does faster mean less real?

The tools don't define the work. The creator does.

The AI doesn't care what you call it. It doesn't care about anything. But you care. How you name the process shapes how you show up to it. It sets the tone for whether you approach the work as a chore or an invitation, whether you rush to extract answers or stay long enough to uncover something more.

That distinction matters.

There's no rulebook for authorship anymore, if there ever was one. For me, it always comes back to this: authorship isn't about how many keystrokes you logged. It's about standing by the work, choosing what stays and what goes, not because it's perfect, but because it's true enough to share.

You could use AI to generate a dozen drafts. You could spin up variations in every voice imaginable. But only you can feel when the tone is off. Only you can say, *This is it. This sounds like me.*

That moment — that decision — is the essence of authorship.

The tools will keep evolving. The technologies will change faster than we can keep up. But the creative process? That part is still ours. Paying attention. Staying curious. Knowing when to trust the spark and when to walk away. Learning how to listen better. That hasn't changed.

AI can mirror your tone. It can draft something quickly. But it can't tell you what matters. It can't tell you where the heat is, where the breath is, where the line hits a little too close in the best possible way.

That's still your job.

Thank goodness for that.

Because the real work — the slow, stubborn labor of shaping something that carries meaning — is still human work. AI might offer you a sentence, a paragraph, or a clean close. But only you can stand behind it and say, *Yes. That sounds like me. That feels like my truth.*

Seeds for Introspection

These aren't tasks to finish. They're places to linger.

- What part of your process feels most fully yours — no matter what tools you use?

- Where are you tempted to hand off authority, and how can you reclaim it?

- Describe a time when staying patient made the work stronger.

- What old beliefs about "real" creativity are you ready to let go of?

- How do you know when a piece of your work feels alive — not just complete?

- What happens in your process when you listen longer than is comfortable?

- How do you define authorship for yourself — not for the marketplace, but for the maker?

- What kinds of presence do your tools reflect back to you?

In the Stillness

The house softens into evening. Outside, a few gulls throw their voices across the water. Nothing urgent. Just presence, circling the sky.

This late in the book, I expected resolution. A clear takeaway. But what I've come to understand is that real learning isn't always neat. It doesn't wrap up on the last page. It echoes. It leaves something behind that keeps working on you long after the writing's done.

This chapter may have sharpened my thinking, but the stillness reminds me that it's the reflection — the part that comes after the effort — where the integration happens. The insight doesn't always show up while you're shaping. Sometimes it arrives when your hands are finally still.

8 The Ongoing Conversation

Finishing a book feels less like crossing a finish line and more like stepping quietly into another beginning. There's a breath of stillness — a pause long enough to admire what you've made — but the work itself doesn't end. It shifts. It changes shape. It invites you to keep moving, not toward perfection or applause, but deeper into the conversation you've already started with your creativity.

What began as a way to write with AI — to shape a book without losing my voice — has stretched into something much bigger. The rhythm I built, slow and stubborn and deliberate, now reaches far beyond the page. It's in how I think. How I create. How I let the day unfold. It's in the pauses, the practices, the small choices that tether me to myself when everything else gets loud.

The work doesn't close with the last paragraph. It simply changes the way the conversation sounds.

What surprised me most wasn't the output — the words, the drafts, the polished pages. It was what stayed with me in the quiet after: the deeper rhythm. The one that doesn't care about word count or grammar. The one that reminds me to return — again and again — with less pressure and more presence.

Working with AI taught me something I didn't expect: creative dialogue isn't reserved for books or paintings or anything that can be held up and finished. It's not a one-time collaboration that ends when you hit "save."

It's a way of moving through uncertainty — with curiosity, with a touch more gentleness.

The AI never dictated what I made. It couldn't. It didn't know what I meant, and it never will. But it served as a willing, wordless partner — mirroring my questions back to me, quietly nudging me to ask better ones. In doing that, it reshaped the way I approach every creative process. Not as something to conquer, but as something to stay in conversation with.

That rhythm follows me now, in ways that feel both ordinary and sacred. It shows up when I'm planting a garden without knowing what will thrive. It's there when I step in front of a canvas, brush in hand, trusting the shape will come. It shows up in the way I patch meals together from whatever's on hand, letting intuition do what the recipe never quite could.

Even in the stillest parts of the day — when the sun is inching its way down behind the hills, or the breeze shifts just slightly across the doorway — that rhythm is there. Ask. Shape. Reflect. Return.

The book may be done. But the conversation — with the work, with the questions, with myself — keeps unfolding.

It would be easy to think of AI as something practical, confined to productivity. A tool for writing tasks, editing lists, outlining the next thing. But when I stopped treating it like a shortcut and started treating it like a mirror, it became something else. Not smarter. Not magical. Just *steadier* than my own distractions.

Now, I reach for it in more places. Not because I need perfect sentences, but because it slows me down just enough to hear myself think. I use it when I'm circling an idea that won't land. I let it sketch a map when I don't know where I'm headed. Sometimes it offers a line I never would've thought of — not because it's profound, but because it bumps me out of my own patterns.

Sometimes it offers something clunky, flat, or way off. But, come on, even that helps. It reminds me where the edge is, where my voice lives. What I'm not willing to compromise. It's not a collaborator in the traditional sense. But it's a presence. A container. A reflection.

The best tools don't do the work for you. They let you stay close to it longer. Long enough to see what might've bloomed if you hadn't rushed away.

That's what this tool has become for me. Not a way to finish faster, but a way to stay in relationship with the work when I might otherwise drift. It holds the thread until I'm ready to pick it up again. It doesn't care if I'm amazing. It just waits for my next input..

Somehow, that waiting — that quiet neutrality — makes me braver. Makes me more honest. Helps me stay in the discomfort long enough to say something true to my heart..

What began as a practical method — "finish the castor oil book with this tool" — became something much more personal. A rhythm I carry into all the places where creativity stirs. Whether I'm writing a new chapter or repotting a stubborn plant, I find myself moving through the same cycle: ask, shape, reflect, return.

It doesn't matter if the work is artistic, domestic, relational, or spiritual. The rhythm stays. It's there when I sketch out a plan. It's there when I walk away from it. It's there when I circle back with a quieter heart.

Yes, AI has a role in that rhythm. Not the main act — just a steady, shadowed presence in the wings. I don't lean on it for answers. I lean on it to hold space for the questions I haven't finished asking. The ones I'm still living into.

It doesn't push. It doesn't rush. It doesn't demand. It doesn't belittle.

That, to me, is the real magic — not efficiency, but endurance. Not shortcuts, but a longer tether back to myself, without fear.

I used to think of creative work as something I had to schedule. Plan. Finish. Now I know it's something I carry. It shows up in conversations I didn't expect to feel so engaging. In the clatter of dishes. In the pull toward the easel, even when I don't know what I'll paint. It's in the moments I'm not trying. The ones I'm just present for.

There's no performance in it anymore. No proving. Just the quiet work of staying connected to what's real — even when it's messy, even when it's half-formed, even when it's nothing more than a small tug in the chest.

AI didn't give me that. It didn't invent my patience. It helped me recognize the pace I was already working in — and stop treating it like a flaw. It wasn't chaos. It was mine. The unfinished essay. The half-painted canvas. The overgrown garden. These aren't signs of failure. They're signs of ongoing conversation. Progress.

This isn't just a method for creating. It's a way of living. A way of meeting the day without needing to have it all mapped out. A way of saying: I'm here. I'm listening. Let's try this again.

Really, that's all the creative life really asks of us. Not brilliance. Not speed. Just the willingness to stay in the frame with the mystery.

To ask again. To shape what we can. To reflect on what we learn. Then to return, not because it's easy, but because it's breathing.

There's no final project that ties everything together. No neat bow at the end. There's only the rhythm.

When you give yourself over to that rhythm — when you let it shape the way you paint, write, speak, parent, love — you begin to see that creativity isn't what you make. It's how you stay.

Seeds for Introspection

Before you dive in: These aren't tasks. They're quiet doors you're invited to lean against, to listen before you step through.

- Where in your life are you being invited to listen longer, not rush ahead?

- What would happen if you treated creative work as an unfolding, not a finish line?

- Where might AI support your creativity without stealing the steering wheel?

- How could you apply the rhythm of ask, shape, reflect, return to non-writing projects — to gardens, to paintings, to conversations?

- What's one project you may have abandoned too soon — and what might happen if you returned to it now?

- Where have you overlooked a quiet, unfinished piece of work that might still be waiting for you?

- How would your creative rhythm change if you stopped measuring progress by speed?

69

In the Stillness

Some evenings, when the sky blends itself into the water and the bay softens under the last light, I sit by the open doors and watch. From a distance, it all looks still. But if you stay long enough, you notice the shifts.

The tide tugs a little farther up the sand. The water deepens its color by small degrees. Dolphins slip through the far channel, almost invisible against the folding light.

None of it happens in a rush. None of it demands your attention. But if you stay, you'll see it: the quiet ways the shoreline reshapes itself. Grains of sand carried in, carried out. Paths rewritten under the surface, unseen but certain.

That's what the creative life feels like now. Not fixed. Not final. Not finished. But moving steadily, quietly, toward what it's meant to become.

I don't control it. I grow alongside it.

If the shoreline can trust the slow, constant revision, maybe I can too.

An Introduction to Artificial Intelligence (AI)

What AI Is (Without the Jargon)

Artificial Intelligence — or AI, if we're keeping it friendly — sounds heavier than it really is. Strip away the headlines and the high-gloss language, and it's surprisingly simple: AI is a way to teach machines how to spot patterns and make educated guesses.

It's not mind-reading. It's not magic. It's a faster, broader kind of pattern recognition. When people hear "AI," they often imagine cold, metallic robots plotting in secret labs or machines cranking out novels while we sip tea and watch the world spin faster. In reality, AI is already stitched into daily life, and it's not as glamorous as the movies make it seem. It's the voice suggesting the next song you might like. It's the spell-check catching your typos. It's the GPS rerouting you when you miss your turn. It's even the predictive text guessing the next word as you type.

AI doesn't think or feel. It doesn't get excited when you have a good idea. It can't sense your frustration when the words don't come. It doesn't wonder what makes a sentence beautiful or a phrase land just right. What it does — extremely well and extremely fast — is recognize massive amounts of patterns: words, numbers, images, behaviors. Based on what it has seen before, it guesses what might come next. It's relentless. It's efficient. But it's not alive.

It can remix. It can reframe. It can fill in blanks you didn't even know were there. But it can't breathe life into anything. That part — the soul part — stays human.

That matters. Because in all the buzz and marketing noise, it's easy to forget: intelligence doesn't equal awareness. AI can be smart without being sentient. It can be impressive without being intentional. It can mimic understanding without ever actually "getting it."

That doesn't make it useless. It just means we need to remember what we're working with — and what we're not.

A (Very) Brief History of AI

AI isn't some brand-new invention cooked up by Silicon Valley. The idea has been simmering since the 1950s, when a few dreamers in lab coats started wondering aloud whether machines could ever think like humans. The first versions were rudimentary — programs that could play a decent game of checkers or solve math problems within a tight set of rules. Not flashy, but the seed was there.

Progress was slow at first. For decades, AI hovered in the background, advancing in fits and starts. It turns out teaching a machine to "think" — even in the simplest way — is a lot harder than it looks in the movies.

What changed everything? Two things: more computing power and more data. As computers got cheaper and faster, and the internet gave us more information than we knew what to do with, researchers started feeding these systems mountains of examples. That's when machine learning entered the scene — a way of training machines not by telling them what to do, but by showing them enough examples that they start to recognize patterns on their own.

Instead of programming strict rules, we gave them raw material: books, articles, photos, songs, code, conversations, maps. The machines didn't become brilliant. They became familiar. They noticed what we repeated. They mirrored us back to ourselves.

Language models like ChatGPT — the kind helping shape this very book — weren't programmed with facts. They were trained on massive libraries of text and designed to predict, word by word, what comes next in a sentence. Not from memory. From probability. It's a little like sitting across from someone who's read every book in the world but hasn't lived a day outside the library.

Useful? Yes. Magical? No. Conscious? Definitely not.

What AI Is (And Isn't)

Let's draw the lines clearly. AI is a fast, capable pattern-spotter. It's a remix artist who never tires. It's a tool that can help spark ideas, organize your thoughts, and offer options when you feel stuck.

It's not sentient. It doesn't know you're there. It won't celebrate when you find your rhythm, and it won't flinch if you throw the whole draft away. It's not creative in the way humans are creative. It can generate, but it doesn't generate meaning.

It can also be hilariously wrong. It might offer confident answers that make no sense at all. It might fabricate facts. It might give you something that *looks* good on the surface but lacks the heartbeat underneath.

Think of AI like a helpful intern with no emotional intelligence. Great with spreadsheets. Terrible with nuance. It can list ten ways to describe your main character, but it won't know which one matches the arc you're building. It can summarize your essay, but it won't understand what made it worth writing in the first place.

It doesn't have intuition. It doesn't have instinct. It doesn't have that strange internal knowing — the flicker in your gut that tells you when a line is right or a color is off. It can reflect your tone, but it can't feel it. It doesn't know what hope tastes like. It doesn't understand grief. It doesn't dream.

But it can still be helpful — especially when you use it as a reflection tool, not a replacement for your own voice. It can hold the space long enough for you to hear yourself more clearly. In a world that rushes everything, that's a gift.

Why This Matters to Creators

For those of us who build — whether that's books, paintings, gardens, businesses, or lives that feel a little more like ourselves — AI can stir up complicated feelings. It's new. It's fast. Let's be honest: it's a little intimidating.

Will it replace us? Will it flatten the weirdness and warmth that makes creative work feel alive?

Here's the truth: AI can give you a clean draft. It can organize your ideas. It can echo your tone once you've taught it well enough. But it can't create resonance. It can't hand you the ache that lives inside a real story. It can't translate longing into lyrics. It can't turn your memories into metaphors. It can't feel what you're trying to say — and it can't help you say it better unless *you* know what you're trying to say in the first place.

Used well, AI can help you stay at work a little longer. It can keep you moving through creative tangles. It can sharpen a paragraph. But it can't replace your point of view. Honestly, that's the part people come for.

The question for creators isn't, "Will AI take over?" The better question is, "Can I stay true to what matters while using this tool to support the process?"

That's where the magic lives. Not in avoiding the tool, and not in surrendering to it — but in learning how to use it without giving up the grit and the grace that make your work yours.

A Quiet Revolution (And How to Stay Human)

There's no denying it — AI is changing the way we work, write, and create. But creativity has always outlived its tools. We've moved from cave walls to canvas to code. The spark has stayed.

AI may stretch the canvas, but it doesn't fill it. It can suggest. It can shape. It can support. But it can't stand in for the part of you that notices the way your dog shifts in the sunbeam or how the air smells before a storm. It can't be moved by a sentence. It can't tell when the shape of a story finally lands.

The world will keep spinning faster. Tech will get sleeker. But the real work of noticing — of turning raw experience into something someone else can feel — that will never be automated. Not really.

The best way to use AI isn't to race it. It's to *stay human while you use it.* Stay weird. Stay slow. Stay honest. Stay close to your questions.

This isn't about keeping up. It's about keeping *close* — to the work, to yourself, to the heartbeat that got you here in the first place.

A Glossary for Creators Working with AI

No big words. No tech-speak. Just a friendly guide to help you feel less lost if AI or creative terms start sounding to hard to grasp..

AI (Artificial Intelligence)

A computer that learns by looking at tons of examples. It doesn't think like a person — it just guesses what should come next.

Algorithm

A set of steps a computer follows to solve a problem. Like a recipe for math.

API (Application Programming Interface)

A way for apps and tools to talk to each other. You don't need to code to use it.

Authorship

Taking credit — and responsibility — for what you create.

Automation

Letting a machine handle repetitive tasks for you. Helpful, but still your ideas.

Beta Version

A test version of software. Not perfect, but almost there.

Bias (in AI)

When the AI repeats unfair ideas it picked up from what it learned. Not on purpose — it just doesn't know better unless we teach it.

Bookmark

A way to save your place — in your browser, a book, or anywhere you want to come back to.

ChatGPT

A chatbot you can talk to. It doesn't understand feelings, but it's good at guessing what might help.

Cloud Storage

Saving your files online so you can reach them from anywhere. Needs Wi-Fi.

Co-creation

Working together — with a person, a tool, or even a bot.

Compression

Making a big file smaller so it's easier to send or save.

Context

The background that gives something meaning. Helps AI stay on track.

Copy (in publishing)

The written words in your book, ad, or website.

Dashboard

The control panel in an app or program. Where all your tools live.

Dataset

The big pile of stuff an AI learned from — books, photos, websites, all kinds of input.

Deep Learning

A way AI learns from lots and lots of examples. Practice, but at lightning speed.

Description (Metadata)

A short summary that helps people find and understand your work.

Draft

The first version of something. Doesn't need to be pretty — it's a starting place.

Embedding

A way to turn words into numbers so computers can use them. Sounds fancy, works quietly.

Engagement

When people interact with your work — like reading, sharing, or commenting.

Feedback

Helpful thoughts from someone else about your work. Doesn't have to be fancy to be useful.

Fine-tuning

Extra training that helps an AI model sound more like you.

Formatting

Lining everything up to look good on the page — titles, spacing, structure.

Generative AI

An AI that can create things — like writing, art, or music — based on your instructions.

Hallucination (in AI)

When AI makes something up and says it confidently. It's not lying — just guessing wrong.

Hashtag

A word or phrase with a # in front that helps people find related posts or topics online.

Hyperlink

A clickable link that takes you to another website or page.

Interface

The part of the screen or tool you use. If it's easy to use, you've got a good one.

Iteration

Trying again, but better each time. A creative do-over.

Keyword

Words people search for. Good for helping folks find your work online.

Language Model

The AI brain that understands and generates text. ChatGPT is one of these.

LLM (Large Language Model)

A really big AI tool trained on a mountain of words. Smart, but still just guessing.

Machine Learning

How computers learn from patterns and slowly get better at guessing what to do.

Metadata

Extra info about your work — like the title, author name, and keywords.

MidJourney

An AI tool that makes images from words. You type what you want to see, and it draws.

Mockup

A preview or draft version of how something will look, like a book cover.

Natural Language Processing (NLP)

The part of AI that lets it understand and use everyday words.

OpenAI

The group that made ChatGPT and other smart tools.

Parameters

Settings that help guide what the AI does and how it responds.

PDF (Portable Document Format)

A file type that keeps its look no matter what device you open it on.

Prompt

What you type in to get the AI started. A question, a sentence, or even a feeling.

Prompt Engineering

Learning how to ask better questions so you get better answers from AI.

Publishing

Sharing your work with the world — online, in print, or however you want.

Query

A question — especially one typed into search or asked of the AI.

Rendering (Visual Tools)

Turning your idea into a picture using AI.

Resolution (Images)

How clear or sharp a picture is. High resolution means more detail.

Rewriting

Using AI to help you revise something you wrote. Still your idea — just reshaped.

Scaffolding

A loose structure or outline to help you build a creative project.

SEO (Search Engine Optimization)

Helping your work show up when people search online. A little structure goes a long way.

Spam (Online)

Unwanted or junky messages — often ads or scams.

Syntax

The way words are arranged in a sentence. AI usually gets it right, but you decide when it *feels* right.

Template

A ready-made format you can fill in. Like a skeleton for your project.

Thumbnail

A small preview image, like for a video or article.

Token

A small chunk of a sentence — sometimes just a word, sometimes less. AI reads in these bits.

Training

Feeding examples to the AI to help it learn. Like study time for robots.

Update

When a tool or app gets new features or fixes. Like a tune-up for your tech.

Upload

Sending a file from your device to the internet. Like putting your work in the cloud's mailbox.

Version

A specific form of a tool, file, or draft. Each version is just one stop on the way to the final thing.

Viral

When something spreads really super fast online. Usually fun, sometimes frustrating.

Voice

The part of your creativity that sounds like *you*. Your style, your rhythm, your truth.

Web App

An online program you use in a browser (like Chrome or Safari), not something you download.

Workflow

The step-by-step way you move through a task or project. Everyone has their own rhythm.

XML (Extensible Markup Language)

A way computers format and share data. You might see it when working with publishing files, but don't worry — you don't need to speak XML to write a book.

YouTube

A video-sharing platform — great for tutorials, storytelling, or getting inspired by others' work. Also where hours go missing.

Zip File

A way to pack several files into one smaller file. Like bundling socks into a drawer — neat and tidy.

THE CREATOR'S RHYTHM

A SIMPLE FLOW FOR REAL WORK WITH AI

PROMPT

Start with what's alive.
Ask a real question.

↓

RESPOND

See what the tool gives you.
Stay curious.

↓

REFINE

Shape what's there.
Keep what feels true.

↓

RETURN

Come back with fresh eyes.
Stay close to your voice.

Use this rhythm in any project that needs presence,
patience, and your true voice.

Where to Keep Exploring

Tools, platforms, and ideas that might support your own creative path.

Helpful Tools & Platforms

These supported this project — and might support yours, too.

ChatGPT

A conversational AI tool for brainstorming, drafting, and shaping creative ideas.

Reedsy

A self-publishing platform with free formatting templates and access to freelance editors and designers.

Canva

A visual design tool that makes creating book covers, promo graphics, or vision boards approachable.

MidJourney

An image-generation platform. Great for inspiration, mood-setting, or visual experimentation.

KDP – Kindle Direct Publishing

Amazon's portal for publishing your work — both in print and digitally.

Squarespace

An intuitive platform for building websites, portfolios, or creative storefronts.

Prompts Starter Kit (Writing with AI)

A simple guide to help you write with AI in a way that feels natural and collaborative.

Recommended Reading

Some books are useful. Others become companions. These tend to do both.

The Creative Act by Rick Rubin

A minimalist meditation on the act of creating, from a legendary music producer.

Big Magic by Elizabeth Gilbert

A joyful, unpretentious look at creative living — fear, failure, and all.

Deep Work by Cal Newport

A field guide to focused, meaningful work in a world that wants to distract you.

A Final Note on the Reading List

These books didn't build this one — they just happen to walk nearby. *Still Human* was shaped by lived experience, long afternoons, and the slow rhythm of figuring things out the unglamorous way.
The titles shared here aren't sources. They're just fellow travelers — books others have found meaningful.

Take what speaks to you. Leave the rest behind, no guilt needed.

Afterword

Just Us Now

If you've made it this far, thank you. Not just for reading, but for walking this with me. This was never meant to be a traditional book. It was a conversation. A rhythm. A lived thing. I'm still surprised by how much life it holds.

When I first started using AI, I didn't plan to write about it. I was in the middle of other books — castor oil, rosemary, aloe vera — and using AI mostly to untangle outlines or fix clunky lines. It wasn't mystical. It wasn't especially smooth. But it helped. And over time, I realized it wasn't just helping me write — it was helping me listen. To myself. To the work. To the rhythm beneath it all.

That's where this book really started, not from a need to explain a tool, but from the pull to share a process. A creative practice I didn't expect to love — and now can't imagine working without.

This wasn't about tech. Or productivity. Or getting faster. It was about something older — the voice I almost lost, and the slow trust it took to return to it.

If anything here gave you a little more permission — to be honest, to stay present to sound like yourself — I'm grateful.

And if you're just beginning to find your own rhythm, here's what I can offer: you don't have to rush. You don't have to smooth down your edges. Just return. As many times as you need to.

That's what I'll be doing too.

With all my gratitude,

—Lisa

About the Author

Rev. Lisa C. Coleman lives off-grid in Baja California Sur, in a place she and her husband Brian call Sanctuary — where sea birds cross the sky, fishermen drift through the channel, and the wind knows how to listen. From this stretch of wild coastline, she writes and publishes books that feel like quiet companions: natural remedy guides, soulful nonfiction, children's stories, puzzles, and coloring pages that offer more breath than instruction.

Lisa is the founder of Laughing Gulls Books, a mother and grandmother, and a survivor in more ways than one. She has walked through cancer, lives with MS, and carries the quiet ache of having lost her entire immediate family to autoimmune disease. That history doesn't define her work, but it gives it weight — a kind of lived-in steadiness that comes from loss, and a willingness to keep showing up anyway.

What she creates isn't about polish or performance. It's about staying present. Her books invite the reader to return to their own voice, their own rhythm — gently, honestly, and without rushing. Whether she's exploring the benefits of castor oil or reflecting on the creative process, her work offers a kind of companionship that doesn't try to fix, but rather to walk alongside.

You can find more of her writing — and a glimpse into life in Baja — at ourbajalife.com.

A Few Gentle Reminders

• AI is a tool, not a muse.

• You are not your output; you are your attention.

• Creativity isn't a race — it's a way back to yourself.

• Progress is presence.

• Your voice is not optional — it's the point.

• Polished doesn't always mean honest.

• Showing up matters more than showing off.

• Let it be messy before it becomes meaningful.

• The tools will keep changing. You don't have to.

• A good draft listens as much as it speaks.

• You don't need to sound like everyone else to be heard.

• Real isn't the same as perfect. It's better.

• Let your questions lead more than your answers.

• Don't rush past the part where you're still becoming.

• The work won't always feel magical. That doesn't mean it's not working.

• Returning is its own kind of success.

www.ingramcontent.com/pod-product-compliance
Lightning Source LLC
Chambersburg PA
CBHW072046040426
42447CB00012BB/3038